Rookie
Read-About®
American
Symbols

The Statue of Liberty

by Lisa M. Herrington

Content Consultant
Nanci R. Vargus, Ed.D.
Professor Emeritus, University of Indianapolis

Reading Consultant
Jeanne Clidas, Ph.D.
Reading Specialist

Children's Press®
An Imprint of Scholastic Inc.
New York Toronto London Auckland Sydney
Mexico City New Delhi Hong Kong
Danbury, Connecticut

Library of Congress Cataloging-in-Publication Data
Herrington, Lisa M.
The Statue of Liberty/by Lisa M. Herrington.
    pages cm. — (Rookie read-about American symbols)
Includes bibliographical references and index.
ISBN 978-0-531-21565-4 (library binding: alk. paper) — ISBN 978-0-531-21838-9 (pbk.: alk. paper)
  1. Statue of Liberty (New York, N.Y.)—Juvenile literature. 2. New York (N.Y.)—Buildings, structures,
etc.—Juvenile literature. I. Title.

F128.64.L6H46 2014
974.7'1—dc23   2014015036

Produced by Spooky Cheetah Press
Design by Keith Plechaty

© 2015 by Scholastic Inc.

All rights reserved. Published in 2015 by Children's Press, an imprint of Scholastic Inc.

Printed in China 62

SCHOLASTIC, CHILDREN'S PRESS, ROOKIE READ-ABOUT®, and associated logos are
trademarks and/or registered trademarks of Scholastic Inc.

5 6 7 8 9 10 R 24 23 22 21 20 19 18

Photographs © 2015: Alamy Images: 24 (Kuttig - Travel - 2), cover (Patrick Batchelder); AP
Images: 12 (Agence Papyrus), 29 right (Mary Altaffer); Getty Images: 29 left (Dirck Halstead/
Liaison), 19 (Don Emmert/AFP); National Park Service, Statue of Liberty NM: 23; Shutterstock, Inc.:
20, 31 center bottom (Aeypix), 20 inset, 31 bottom (Chris Parypa Photography), 31 top (gary718),
4, 31 center top (Sean Pavone), 3 bottom (Xavier Marchant); Superstock, Inc./age fotostock: 27;
The Granger Collection: 7 (Rue des Archives), 11, 15, 16, 28 left, 28 right; The Image Works/Albert
Harlingue/Roger-Viollet: 8; Thinkstock/Luciano Mortula: 3 top.

Illustration by Jeffrey Chandler/Art Gecko Studios!.

Scholastic Inc., 557 Broadway, New York, NY 10012.

Table of Contents

Meet Lady Liberty

The Statue of Liberty stands high above the waters off New York City. The statue is a **symbol** of freedom. It is also called Lady Liberty. Liberty means freedom.

The Statue of Liberty is located on Liberty Island in New York Harbor.

Long ago, people from other countries came to live in the United States. They dreamed of freedom. They wanted a better life. The Statue of Liberty welcomed them as they arrived on ships.

FUN FACT!

The statue's full name is *Liberty Enlightening the World.*

8

The beautiful statue was a gift from France. It honored the friendship between France and the United States. A French artist designed the statue. His name was Frédéric-Auguste Bartholdi.

FUN FACT!

Bartholdi is said to have used his mother's face as the model for the statue.

Building the Statue

In 1875, workers in France started to build the giant statue. They hammered thin sheets of metal to make the outside of the statue. The metal they used was copper.

FUN FACT!

When the statue was built, it was the color of a copper penny. Over time, the copper turned green from being outside.

First the workers built a strong frame to hold the statue up. It was made of iron. Then the frame was covered with the copper pieces.

FUN FACT!

Alexandre-Gustave Eiffel designed the inside frame for the Statue of Liberty. He later built the Eiffel Tower in France.

The statue was shipped to America in 350 pieces.

Workers spent nine years building the statue. In 1884, it was finally finished. The statue was taken apart in 1885. It was packed in 214 boxes. A boat carried the boxes to America.

FUN FACT!

The Statue of Liberty weighs 225 tons (204 tonnes). That is about as much as 45 elephants!

15

In 1886, the statue was put together in New York. It was placed on a stone **pedestal**. The pedestal had been made in America.

Lady Liberty stands 305 feet (93 meters) tall. That is as high as a 22-story building. At the time, it was the tallest statue in the world.

Crowds celebrate at the statue's opening ceremony on October 28, 1886.

Symbols of the Statue

The different parts of the Statue of Liberty have special meaning. The crown has seven spikes. They stand for Earth's seven seas and continents.

Visitors can see New York City from the crown's windows.

torch

The tablet's date is written in Roman numerals.

In her right hand, Lady Liberty raises a **torch**. The torch is a symbol of freedom. In her left hand, Lady Liberty holds a **tablet** with July 4, 1776, written on it. That is America's birthday.

FUN FACT!

In 1986, Lady Liberty was repaired for her 100th birthday. Among the changes was a shiny new torch.

The Statue of Liberty steps out of broken chains at her feet. The broken chains also stand for America's freedom from Great Britain.

FUN FACT!

Inside the pedestal is a museum where visitors can learn how the statue was made.

Seeing the Statue

Each year, millions of people visit the Statue of Liberty. They can read a famous poem about freedom. Emma Lazarus wrote the poem. It was added to the pedestal in 1903.

FUN FACT!

The Statue of Liberty was first used as a lighthouse.

The poem gives a voice to Lady Liberty. Its words capture what the statue meant for the millions of people who came to America for freedom. Part of the poem says:

Give me your tired, your poor,
Your huddled masses yearning to
breathe free...

The Statue of Liberty is one of the most famous symbols in the world.

1875
Work on the statue begins in France.

1886
A big ceremony takes place to open Lady Liberty.

1884
The statue is completed in France.

1885
The statue is shipped in pieces to America.

1986
The Statue of Liberty celebrates her 100th birthday.

2013
The statue reopens. It was closed after Hurricane Sandy hit the area in 2012.

1903
Emma Lazarus's poem is placed on the pedestal.

The Statue of Liberty

The statue's new torch is covered in thin sheets of gold. The original torch is on display inside the statue.

There are 25 windows in the crown.

The face on the Statue of Liberty measures more than 8 feet (2.44 meters) tall.

The statue's copper covering is very thin. It is less than the thickness of two pennies!

There are 354 steps from the pedestal to the head of the Statue of Liberty.

JULY
IV
DCCLXXVI

Glossary

pedestal (PED-i-stuhl): the base of the statue

symbol (SIM-buhl): an object or design that stands for something else

tablet (TAB-lit): a piece of stone with writing on it

torch (torch): a flaming light that can be carried or mounted on a wall

Index

Facts for Now

Visit this Scholastic Web site for more information on
the Statue of Liberty:
www.factsfornow.scholastic.com
Enter the keywords **Statue of Liberty**

About the Author

Lisa M. Herrington writes books and articles for kids. She lives in
Trumbull, Connecticut, with her husband, Ryan, and daughter,
Caroline. She climbed to the crown when she first visited the Statue
of Liberty on a class trip in high school.